Men in the Nude in Socks
and Other Poems

Richard Swanson

FIREWEED
PRESS

P.O. Box 482
Madison, WI 53701-0482

Men in the Nude in Socks

Printed in the United States of America
by Inkwell Printers, Dodgeville, Wisconsin
for Fireweed Press

ACKNOWLEDGMENTS:

Thanks to the following publications, in which versions of some of these poems have appeared: "Morning, the Sun Nudging You Into a Yawn," *Beloit Poetry Journal*; "Little Girl Drowned," *Blue Unicorn*; "The Poet's Tell-all," *California Quarterly*; "Bear," *Fox Cry Review*; "Grammar Basic," *Kansas English*; "Young Teen Girls Saying Good-bye," *Mobius*; "Next Door," *Passager*; "Insomnia: A Documentary," *Piedmont Literary Review*; "Men In the Nude in Socks," *Rockford Review*; "Last Renaissance Sonnet Self-Destructs," *Tributary*; "Grand Opera," *TriQuarterly*; "An Afternoon Among the Politically Famous; *Wayne Literary Review*; "Vietnam Moratorium," *We Speak for Peace*; "Volunteer Fire Department," *Wisconsin Academy Review*; "Degas Dancers," *Wisconsin People and Ideas*; "Ducky," *Wisconsin Poets' Calendar, 2006*; "Dissertation: Love as Compost," *Wisconsin River Valley Journal*, "Great White Dove Hunter," *Wisconsin Review*. "Wishes for the Next War" won third place in the Nuclear Age Peace Foundation contest for 2004 and was published at that organization's Web site. "Grand Opera" was also published on-line at Poetry Daily.

Cover design by Jack Ford

Special thanks to Robin Chapman, Jeri McCormick, Richard Roe and Lynn Patrick Smith for their thorough, perceptive editing.

ISBN 1-878660-20-9

CONTENTS

OCCASIONS

OBSERVATIONS

AMUSEMENTS

Men in the Nude in Socks

Hey, lookit!

These men in the nude in their socks -
all pinko torso and hatchling-haired legs.
Are those bald spots on the backside
or rumps on top?
Gawd, get a snapshot
get a guffawish gawk at
the gluteus maximus,
the muscle minima.
Remember the member-
ous droop and its stoop-
endous testicular particulars.
Come, let us gaa-gaa this fold-out,
slather our ardor at this
bare-boned dualped planted in argyles.
Observe, observe:

Herr Fashionable Fuzzy Foot,
dimples, moles, flabulous contours,
a haunch to shame the showcase tapestries
of a meat market, oh there's more . . .

No nothing more than the image
of men in the nude in their socks
and the point the image is for:

Men in the nude in socks do not make war.

Symphony for the Common Man, Variation
(A Guide to Recreational Wiring)

He likes the simple way things function,
the black wire mated to black;
the white return, to white.
With the vernal ground-wire screwed down tight
he tries his circuit.

Presto.
Lights, sounds, drama!
He's made an event.
The house hums, he hums, ho-hums his
art with 110 volt spaghetti.
Aw, shucks, 'twarn't nothin,' ma'am.
I been roping steers, tuning cars,
and putting out nuclear meltdowns for decades.

Hey, what's this though? At the workbench junction box
a rubber perfume, no, stench.
And sparks? Bastille day?

No damn cause for celebration,
he thinks, as the breaker pops
and the wife calls down to his cave:
Teddy, you down there? At it again?
They were kissing, right on my soaps.
You got no sense of romance.

No current either
for an hour and another
then just before dinner everything finally works.
He's won. Over a beer he conjures the thing
they'll say when he dies:

He was a man with good connections.

Insomnia: a Documentary

MIDNIGHT

*Just one last thought just
one last laser insight.*

His eyelids remind him to
Sleep now relax now
it's curfew for muscles, bar time for brains

But I'm getting this glimmer.

ONE A.M., FERAL PROWL HOUR

He can light the bedroom murk.
He sees the tenement stairways of the world
neoned with his phosphorous logic.
He can sapper the ills of the earth.

He's up, to a pulse-pump of coffee.

TWO FIFTEEN, GIVE OR TAKE TEN

Who's this Karl Marx/cat burglar/Plato
plotting Utopia over java in the kitchen?

*Why not - yes! - a benefit concert
by under-four prodigies for striking airline pilots?*

THREE

There's a savior in his heart, a war room plan on his table,
a glitch in the man's agenda:

*Uh, oh, the tiny tyke maestros
can't cross airport strike lines
to get to the concert; hence no benefit,
no needed song bucks for the grounded
wind and wing jockeys.*

He's back to year zero of history and bed.

FOUR, BY THE RADIUM DIAL

He'd sleep but his body says no
you invested in the Bank of Ideals,
and here is your payoff:
a run on your neural reserves,
a gyral spine and twitches,
limbs jumpy as lightning,
hot sheets, mauled pillows.

FIRST LIGHT BREAKING

His mind clicks off.
On the trail of a snore, he'll rest now
sleep now, settle like a dune.

Wrong! WAKE Radio,
its Breakfast Roundup,
shells his ears, yanks his eyelids up.

>   *Gotta get going, meeting at ten.*
>   *Can't sleep through it, may have to.*

One foot out on the floor. The other.

Will his limbs work?
The muscles are concrete or cork.

Hey, have a headache on you, yourself, he thinks, gratis.
Maybe the nine-to-five millions slept in this morning.

Groans getting up like a garbage truck in ascendant dump-phase.

Have a nice day, the radio chirps.

Elegy for Ted, in Two Parts
(Ted Williams, in cold storage, head separated from his body)

The wrists, the arms - their whipping grace - which pull
the torso forward, pride of Boston
flowing, fastball cracked and gone, for faithful
fans to cherish - ah, the Ted of legend.
Fenway still remembers. The heartland too.
And you, now dead but just a year, preserved,
a cryogenic freeze and frieze, an icon cool
and calm as always. Such crystalline reserve.

Oh, Ted, a little too detached, you were, they said.
Warm to the day, the pennant in contention.
Uneasy lies your neatly severed head,
unnerved our national conviction.
Pull together, step up square, and home that eye.
Blast the bombers. Let us belt one, you and I.

2002

Grand Opera

Already catastrophe!
In the small peasant village people arise
to Sophie's betrayal of Juan,
her loving intended, in the night.
Juan is loose like a jaguar,
and someone is going to die.

Some vocal ruminations first though.
Sophie: How strange, how voiceless the larks today.
Juan: How hot the fired steel of my rage.

Soon all the villagers gorge on this infidelity.

More songs and crescendos. Three mocking crones
raise howls on stage, as Sophie's new man
croons, falsetto, in transit to the country's borders.

A waft of hope: pleas made, souls excavated
while honor wrestles forgiveness.

Thunderclouds boiling, over the housetops.
Trumpets! Shouts!
All of the villagers gather for blood flow.

Let it happen,
the gushing from chests and bellies.

Grammar Basic
(Lie and Lay, Rules for)

Lie so sprawls, it's downright asnooze,
a hammocky verb at ease:
I *lie*, i.e., *relax, recline.*

Lay is up and needs play:
I *lay* the rose at your dew-brushed feet, dear waif;
the flawless case before you, Judge, Your Honor.

In past tense waters, though, *lie* takes *lay* as twin:
I *lay* (*lie's* yesterday) down in languored, long siesta.
Meanwhile *lay*, the crab, moults form to *laid*:
Dozing, I *laid* the plans for revolution.

Enter *lain*. With *have, lie* sniffs snuff at your local club:
I *have lain* abed in mid-Manhattan
for seven centuries for this very moment.
Meanwhile *lay* is constant:
I have *laid* an egg with my ten last New York revolutions.

Lie, lay, lain;
lay, laid, laid.
Everything clear like royal brandy.

If only there weren't the troubling offspring
cruising in Nounsborough City:
lie: a golfer's nestly launch point,
lay: a troubador's stroll song,
lie: an outright nix-on-you prevarication,
finally, _____, the sordid in-the-sheets (weeds) scoring.

Best to lie low when the overly randy
lay before you the lies of their latest lays.

Tabloid Tale
"Man, Hero, Waits Decades for Highway Collapse"

Boy-eyed, baseball capped, elbows like chicken wing joints,
he watched with friends from a knoll.

There on the highway construction below he saw:
the gap in the mesh in the concrete,
the flaw that could kill.

Downhill he pled to the crew head: Please, sir,
there's a problem.
In your eyesight, Sonny, the hard-hat swaggered.
Mama, he cried, someone could suffer.
Guess who, she countered, if you keep on wasting my time?

So his vigil commenced.
When the highway opened he set up outpost
and trudged to the knoll each day
ready with splints and bandages.

Years yawned away.
Knoll Nothing they'd dubbed him in high school.
By then he'd lost friends but still kept the vision
of a hole leering up in someone's windshield
and children flying, shorn of gravity, to doom.

Agony: the morning he would leave for college
the first of the fissures appeared.
Who would be there with the stretchers?
As he lifted the first of his shirts from the suitcase,
his father appeared: Stop! Re-pack! You will get in the car!

College. A turning?
Four years in two, three more in one, he did, whizzy!
He raced home, though,
took job, wife, residence -

buying the knoll -
and now from his picture window, telescope aimed,
he watched as the fissure widened to cracks.

It took one year.
Then one morning the highway opened, a death gape
swallower of metal and flesh.
But almost before the first flying limbs touched down
he was there with the maimed and shredded.

He raged for the killed but bent to the others.
Here is my hand in your hour of need, he soothed.
As you recover think of me,
and here is my card.
My law firm charges you nothing to sue.

We claim a portion of your winnable verdict.

Barbie, Her Fantasy

Ken, His Nostalgia

Oh to be
sweaty
gin-breathed   Now, no
braless   back when:
bucked up   all buff good
high in a   chest arms teeth
Pittsburgh bar,   big bright
a rowdy   float flags
raw teamster   kids on Main Street
trucker   the Caddy on GLIDE
getting his   and fresh waxed
big paw dirty   me there, perched up
nailed fingers   Rotary
deep, deep   head guy
in the roots   waving, smiling:
of my all   Ken, Ken, Ken!
let loose and
just go scummy
blonde hair.

Idiot's Guide to Dummies

Know them for head nods when five
sidles in as two plus two,

for their ready salutes for duty
in the regiment ranks of hype and drivel.

That's them too, whoop dee do,
at yesterday's Mother Teresa sighting.

Mourning a furry lost loved one,
the Smiths have named their new daughter Spot.

Darwin, the crude long pageant of you and me
before him, scratched his frothed brain

over how this aberrant species lurched forward.
No such worry ever fretted its members.

In Each Other's Cross-hairs

I got this gun to save me
from my next door neighbor who
says I'm crazy and has all these guns,
which drives me crazy
and makes me buy guns.
I'm not crazy, it's you,
I tell him you're nuts for
having those guns,
but not if you're neighbor, says he,
to someone like you with
all those guns, that's . . .

Keats Lite

You and your girlfriend find this old glazed vase
and, hey, on one of its sides this young Greek couple
frisks around doing what you'd do
in a nearby woods, this weekend.
He's on her heels, she runs coy, but IT
doesn't happen. Can't. 'Cause they're
freeze-framed ceramic. Not good, bad story:
Guy doesn't get girl.

Wait. Think. He'll always be hot and hers truly,
this way, for a thousand years
while she'll be young forever with damselly ankles
and an extra virgin come-get-me ness.

What a sad song of everyone's almosts,
the pot's sweet flute riffs
of beautiful trade-offs.

Cool confusion.
Connect.

Last Renaissance Sonnet Self-destructs

So much wanting to plight its courtier's
love airs, alas, it's a hackish rhyme bomb.
Music, my servant! the courtier orders.
Ladyward, rousing itself from thromb-

ositic spasm, it de-phlegms its cords,
looses a deep-in-diaphragm, cavernous
gusto as it ventures upscale toward
the high-C registers and wondrous

croaks! Frog notes! Oh, poor thing,
may it finally for always fulfill
one grand wrackurous sing
this moment of a dying fall,

a proper finale-ous fit
to the nth iambic pfft.

NATURAL THINGS

Ducky

Got the scaup scoop,
learned the teal feel, moved
in the best wigeon regions,
got wise with goldeneyes,
gabbed well with gadwalls,
roared with the ruddy rowdies
honkered a ballard with the mallards.

Earned the Order of Shovelier.

Quarreling with Gertrude Stein

So: a rose is a rose is a rose?
the object in question
(the way this goes)
alive by rote repetition?

Moreover, your object in question
in Gertrudian thought
is not just alive by rote repetition
but one most purely wrought?

Alas, in your abstract Gertrudian thought
isn't the rose of our yard!
Ours, in dirt most purely wrought,
in the light it leans toward,

is the Ingrid Bergman rose of our yard,
the object made real.
By the fence, in the light it leans toward,
all its core crimson concealed

this hybrid tea object made real
is a leaf bud bound in
till all its core crimson concealed
unfolds as rapturous sin.

Note, too, from the leaf bud bound in
from the deep, full bore of its bloom
unfolding as rapturous sin
comes upward a freed perfume.

From the deep full bore of the bloom
(the ways this goes)
out and upward comes a freed perfume.
Yes, a rose, we inhale, is a rose is a . . . rose

Great White Dove Hunter

See one, shoot one:
Wild Bill Hick show!

Or gun for food,
a bird per cracker.

Mount one
warm and silky. Stuff it.

When Johnny questions,
lament:

Though your ancestors
braved floods and blizzards,
you might not survive
your pitiful trek
to the backyard gazebo

to blow something away.

Watching Crows Mating

Hate them.
Loathe and revile
them, and while

you do,
they're loving
coving

their heads,
beaks,
necks

in the soft
black
backs

of each other
doing
the wooing

we'd never begin
or dare
compare

to acts
we've grown
to see as ours alone.

Encounter

The lazy and lofty ease of it
up there over pine tops.
The way it let itself lift from
and own every updraft the lake
could free to its wheeling wingspread.
Yet not till it broke from its gyres
and sheered down the sky
white head homed on target
did I take in all, all my breath for it.

My god it was after a loon though
and one on a nest, trapped there
by allegiance to unborn offspring.
I heard in the loon's first sound
as the eagle aimed down on it
almost a keening, the low throat timbre
tremored with fear.

Then the loon joined battle,
mustered up will and screaming
- turned screaming to outrage,
made outrage a weapon:
How dare you, how dare you!
as it heaved itself upward
in awkward wing thrash.

When the eagle broke flight, swerved
from its set trajectory, I saw its action
as feint or cunning, till it showed itself
simply confused and finally just beaten,
marauder sent skyward by the loon's cacophony.

Back in the pine tops, chastened,
the eagle fell back to its wheeling on air.
Once, it tilted an eye back toward the nest,
but the loon, on guard still, saw and replied -
this time a sharp, mean warning turning to
one long croon burst of triumph, a song
so resplendent the whole lake shook with it.

Bear

Wind gusts mean with sleet,
in a charcoal afternoon
I have loped home
from the valley of commerce
to the cave of house
and epidermis of bedroom comforter.

I have left out the groceries

yet something whispers,
Forget them, let down
your eyelids till April
in a drowse as deep as history.
Good.
You simply must have this sleep.

Homage to Thoreau

Homed on the sheen on coins
up at dawn they're out, the manic hundreds
in the Yankee towns of commerce.

Henry rises in Concord, too,
fixed like them on gold but that
in the light on his scuffed up floor.

They want. They yowl and moil:
Coins. Things. Horse and cow stock.
Land and houses and garb and trinkets.
Never enough! Run for them, after them!

Henry leaves town in a shuffly amble
for woods which are there for the taking,
the taking in, more striking for leaving as is.

Din, din diminished but there still
from the left behind mob,
the lemmings chasing the flash of the hour:
The news! Tell! Who's the strut of the day?
What's the cut and tinge of latest fashion?

Henry walks in his coat so thin at the elbows
the seeping in breeze feels like childhood wonder.
He notes the coming out show of gentians,
the tilt in the Jack in the Pulpit's hat brim.

More still, shrill though fading,
the braying mules of the roaring republic,
citizens crazed, lock-stepped off to global zealotry,
the newest hosanna of war: Mexico.

How rousing, thinks Henry, this cannon boom shot
of grouse in a burst from bramble.
Here's his smart salute to the butterfly admirals,
Vanessa atalanta, their hind wing
orange tips flared on thistle stalk.

The pond now, where Oversoul nature beckons:
Sit you down here, Mr. H. D. Thoreau.
Reside and preside as Walden's resident log-master
in the wealth of the morning's comings and goings.

Henry in place, Henry at ease
for the business of hours, the eyeing and earing
of newt, ant, bee, bee in mallow, fern in beech shade,
heron in duck wort, swallow in arc, bass churn,
aspen lisp, wren rant, moth whim, sun caper, grub chaw,
fox stride, bark seep, bream swoosh, the sway of rue anemone.

A splendid, fine day, he thinks, on log's end,
minder of self, woods mayor, owner of all his senses.

Sits. Does nothing. Does nothing exceedingly well.

Next Door

Gerry, his boss and once good friend, takes him aside:
Cutbacks are coming, you should know.

The bill for his pickup's new tires
breathes all night long next to his bedside lamp.

Our kids have everything, he hears himself say,
and almost as much bad judgment.

Mom Jensen still jokes a little: Pills or heat for winter -
blood pressure down but the propane gone. Ha, ha.

Hurt. Wants to. Someone, some day.
Won't. Instead will get in the pickup and drive,

drive out County M till he finds them, the cranes,
the sand-hills, crazy with song on the river flats.

HAPPILY EVER AFTER

NO. 1195 89

NAME:					DATE: 6·23	
ADDRESS:						
CITY, STATE, ZIP						
SOLD BY:	CASH	C.O.D.	CHARGE	ON ACCT.	MDSE RTD.	PAID OUT

QUAN.		DESCRIPTION	AMOUNT	
	1	Saucer R	6	—
	2	Steaming	6	—
	3	The Monkey Collection²	3	95
BW	4	Kai Living	10	—
	5	Fruition Known		
4	6	BB	4	—
	7	Men in the Nude	12	—
	8			
	9		41	95
	10		2	31
	11			
	12		44	26

CUSTOMER'S ORDER NO.	RECEIVED BY:

Morning, the Sun Nudging You into a Yawn

Morning, the sun nudging you into a yawn
then staying to nuzzle your shoulder -
call it Portrait: Woman Waking
or, simply, Dawn,

hardly a name to describe it
with the shrubbery starting to stir
and the curtains catching the air
over a pillow partially sunlit -

much less a title for you.
You breathe steadily,
your hand on your forehead,
brushing aside a hair or two,

and I speak your name.
Outside the sky flexes red,
teasing the foliage to green,
and your calling remains the same.

Now I name you again. Waker-
at-ease and warmth, I call you,
and leaf bud open in hand
of your garden's caretaker.

Love Among the Hors d'oeuvres

He: Kiss me, Love, kiss.
I'm pickled, peppered, cheesy,
a mad monster of marination,
a garlic that withers the cat.
I know the reek of radish and am O
onion oral but, Sweet,
make sweet my breath, Love,
with your lips, Love, lips.

She: You and your acid angst,
your anchovy ardor.
Fish foul, hale as herring.
Mints were meant for these exhalations,
Love, not my lips,
but love is better well seasoned so
kiss me, Love, kiss.

What You See Is What You Get

What you see is what you get,
he said, a me for you,
and only you, un-taken yet.

She swam love's reefs, a male to
make her passionate,
then found a lacy thing, two

sizes small, within his travel kit.
What's this? she posed.
He drawled: You'd best get used to it;

your wiser intuition knows
how jealousy in bed
can leave a husband ill-disposed.

She gaped, she sank, writhed
on corals in the amorous seas,
feared to look on where she'd bled.

How could the never-come-to-be
so quickly happen?
What I got, she wailed, is what I see?

What She Didn't Wake Up to This Morning

Was his sniffing, his humph, his
just above audible huff through his nose
- big boy buffalo coming on through:
Get outta the way, you think you
belong here, though we're married?

Was his forefinger pointing, accusing:
trash lid up, streaks on the mirror,
three missed weeds on the patio,
car seats dusty, and you're late for work,
not that you'd notice.

Was his bull whip snap, his saying
should have, shouldn't have
wrong again, stupid, stupid and dumb and
go get some pink on your cheeks
for your all the time saggy face look,
you joke as a slave you.

Were their neighborly casseroles,
suede soft eyes and hands in condolence,
the voices they thought she'd not hear:
 . . . just not facing his passing and
him so charming so kind so sad and
what on earth will she do?

She will do fine, thank you, she will
starting today in moments called hers
roam the haven of house and silence,
will sit with tea on a sunlit porch while saying
in a giddy but frighted finding of self
He's gone, all gone and buried and oh so away.

Dissertation: Love as Compost

Nothing so good as garbage in a heap
for a languishing garden,
so each of us tossed in our slights to the other,
and crusty grudges, and layered in years
of sticky resentments for chemical verve.

These too: a will to hurt and meanness
(grey potato, black potato).

When we lobbed in too-told jokes and stories,
the cabbagy leaf-rot of flat affections,
the pile gained warmth,
so we pitched in a chile-hot feud
we'd never resolved.

That started it seething.

Damn thing reeks, said a neighbor.
True, it was true.
The worms, our Cold War spies,
had stirred insurrections by microbe cadres.
But then came musk-heavy coolness
from night-rich rains and a fragrant breathing
through the twig twisted cross section.

One morning we woke to a rosy waft
from backyard sources:
old love's fumes we'd made new scents of.

Romantic Inventory

Books all over, money clip, unused fly rods, wayward hair -
his.
Potter's wheel, plants, auburn glasses, a score of bras -
hers.
Some of the sum of the parts of their
house.

The now-quiet house
has leftover hair
in the bath sink (theirs)
which is his,
and something of hers
in their shower: bras.

He parts the half-dozen bras
every day in the shower in the house,
those 34C mesh and cup traps, hers.
They start his day, they get his hair
all corkscrew tight, his jaw jut-taut, his
spine steel stout, those goddamned bras with their

snakish straps and snaps and their, their--!
She hisses that the silken pennants of bras
are much less worse than the comb wads, his
hair in the sink in the bath in the house.
Daily she finds those casseroles of hair
in the bowl, those free-stranded sprouts in her

rouge, his scalp-flakes in everything marked HERS.
Now she knows the meaning of *their*.
Will he never be bald? All this morning hair
makes her skin itch all the way down to her bra.
This is his, not her, way of playing house
so someday with a tweezers she will yank his

hairs, each one, free of his
follicles, yes, squealing, he will be all hers.
Meanwhile his rich-haired skull has housed
a scene of them both together in their
shower, he hoisting her hair by her bras
for once too often getting in his hair.

He and she. His and hers. Bonds. Theirs.
And bondage bound. Just now in their house he lifts her bra
from her breast while she strokes the paths of his hair.

Love Song with Four Banalities

Her seamless Spandex,
his cutting edge rip,
their slippery slope sheets,
her over the top of him

sigh.

Why not you and I?

OCCASIONS

After the Assassination (Martin Luther King, Jr.)

Pomp and tribute, three long days of it,
profile his life-span: birthplace; youthplace;
how he met her, the wife at his walnut side now;
his public days and causes won;
this rupture of shock.

Here are the children soothed by official regrets,
no less salved by his making events
a page in the grand chronology.
The pundits reflect, historians muse.
He's safe in the books to be written.

Exit the camera. The sound truck slinks away
with the last of the on-tape tears,
and his legend begins.
Left in his dust are the living data
to wipe away all mourning.

The shot never happened.
This is the end of senseless acts.

Vietnam Moratorium

They are reading the dead, are reading
the names of the dead in battle tonight
on the soaked cement in one lone spotlight
but mainly in candlelight and under the war black
umbrellas they read the names of Hope Hopmann
Johns Jansen the list they read
is sick with moisture the microphone
coughs with the weather and the people
stand listen do not talk but remember
the dead on the side of the world remote
from this wet small place where the eyes
stare down at the Wagners Watkins Yates Young
dead on the public address tonight as
they read the dead.

1969

Coming Upon Them   (The Gulf War, 1991)

I saw them as statues, a sculpture group
set on a bluff and facing in concert
an open horizon. But that would come later.

First they were there as oddity,
stark bundled forms on a public square
in everyone's way an unmoving presence
but not to be jeered since maybe a
torturing jokester had scissored their tongues,
so still they stood.

Abandoned? Lost? To their thoughts, yes.
QUAKERS STANDING IN SILENCE FOR PEACE
a sign at their feet said.

I edged around them like others,
felt the rushes of easy derision that oddity prompts.
What would they do if the day, one in December,
brought some of their kind to sneezing?
New sign needed: QUAKERS WITH COLDS COMING ON.

But none of them moved or swayed with the weather
as I slowed to observe them fully.

They asked no favors,
just stood to be seen, wordless, their eye-talk clear:
We're better, both you and we, than what we have known
and let strut to folly.
Consider the rightness of acts refused
and things not done.

I left them then but kept coming back
though miles and months away
on the mind's path's strayings.

I'd taken, like them, to artful inertia.

Mandela Free

(Nelson Mandela, freed after having served twenty-five years for political agitation)

Someone unhuddled,
something like conscience uncellared,
stands at the prison-house door,
moves to, blinks from, then uses
the sun's blaze to sort time present from memory.

It's open, the gate,
no joke in a dream but real,
this minute, the last of fourteen million
they shut me in for,
for being the black man's howl
in their septic white streets.

He would like now merely to go to his home,
to touch again, feel anew
the things of his family,
taste smell savor all over
the bread of his kitchen table, but

Not right now, this is a time
for meeting, greeting the faithful,
these hardened, delirious thousands,
who wait this day for the eager press mob
to beam our triumph abroad.

He will say things, thoughts so blandly profound
they merit re-hearing:
Wrongs dressed stylish are still just wrong.
Hopes held down turn anguish to tactics.
Freedom will rise somehow after night-stick beatings.

From his cell he brought down a government.
This morning he will start to make one,
born in his jailed reflections.

Later, some things for myself.

His lungs fill up with new-found air.

Abu Ghraib

Whatever was in the mind
of us? Find it in words!
What does it say of our kind

who practiced a devil's design
there, of torture as cure?
Whatever was in the mind

to think that screams confined
wouldn't be, couldn't be heard?
What does it say of our kind

of vision, that we'd find
through shaming a way to stir
whatever was in the mind

of people outside toward blind,
cold acts of vengeance undeterred?
What does it say of our kind

of stupefied logic, leaving behind
all reason? How absurd,
whatever was in the mind.
What *does* it say of our kind?

Wishes for the Next War

That the dogs of war on the eve of battle
share their fleas with their generals' socks.

That codes of smart bombs be sent to dyslexic pilots,
who drop all their ordnance into the sea.
That tanks on the road to glory return to base
with the hiccups.

That soldiers on opposite sides in separate tents
get sent by scrambled mail
the photos of each others' families.
That field commanders lose interest.
That subsequent orders begin with "If you'd like to . . ."
That maps of battle crumble like manna from heaven.

That the generals dance for peace.
That the checks for weapons bounce.
That vultures starve from lack of spoils.
That the troops sleep in, this morning, tomorrow,
and as long as it suits them,
knowing the sweetness of time on one brief earth.

OBSERVATIONS

Cats in Old Bookstores

Prowling in all these ideas,
chummy with Plato and Mickey Spillane,
they must know something we don't
or just feel calm in our being
bifocaled musers who shuffle along,
harmless in faded Woolrich.

In this small town's Bibliomaniacs
a feline threesome holds casual court,
one just ambling a minute ago
over to History-Mespotamia,
while a second claims all the late-fall sun
along with Virginia Woolf
in the upstairs window alcove.

For the third, a mostly black, part white tom
named Captain, life's a stretch
by the 1950's cash register, and we pay him obeisance,
a behind the ears rub-up, when he sniffs to us,
down on us, though we're above him.
He is (they are) after all, of the worldly wise,
taking the long, lank, soft and supple view.

Degas Dancers

On point, in place
in pliés sprung
with heady grace

the dancers spin
and check and
float again

as if to say
Ignore, ignore
our aired display.

This lift of toe
and tulle, the heights
to which we go

of which we're part
- what little use!
mere breathless art.

Film Noir

Indigo midnight. Post-war Prague.
Fog wisps zephyring pavements.

The street light sulfurs their meeting.

She's all the women he's ever wanted
who just might kill him.
He'll do, she thought once, strictly for hire
but then a candled heart showed, in the private eye.

Enter the jealous husband, the lately-exposed ex-SS officer,
scale-faced in his cigarette's glow,
fondling his Lugar in the shadows as he watches them.
Note the gold from the Jews in his teeth as he leers.

Car lights passing: flit, flit, flit.
A strobe-light rake slashes her face
under the hero's broad-brimmed hat.

Mustn't be seen, mustn't.
But they've touched now, embraced, the very first time.
Stop it, you fools, you'll be –

The Lugar's bolt slides, the husband sights down the barrel

at nothing! But how? They were here, just here!

Light blinds as light illumines.
Dark cloaks as dark discloses.

Who will survive this luminous murk?

Gestation, the 1950s

The first months I dreamed I gave birth to a swimming pool.
I had I suppose an enlarged view of my blown-up body
and was sick a good time.
Later I dreamed such things as ranch style houses
with pretty suburban acres
as the sickness passed.

Then came pink corsages and centerpiece crystal
and small white badges in sunny pavilions.
I think they were large affairs, they were
small white name-tags HELLO
they said MY NAME IS . . .
Hello, the voices would echo, my name is . . .
and smiled I think I remember
I was pleased in those nights before birthing
and urged on myself this thought:

May I deliver if not a ladies' magazine then
a philanthropic project with standing committee
and may it beget agendas at elegant teas
with grapefruit punch.

These things took place in the course of my time,
the reverie good, the bearing a disappointment.

Poverty

We could stop it,
but the blight's on-going.

The mother: half-rooted, a brittled stem at forty,
in youth too striking for speech
but not above striking, in the eyes
of her now-vanished husband.

These were the codes of her late-teen years:
pregnant again, food stamps, keep moving ahead of the rent.
These are the words of a language
she couldn't have known and never will:
cash after payday, man who's faithful, future.

The summer light shifts toward a daughter,
the garden's new growth but a bud leafed out
when the mercury seethes.

She's cute, boy-crazy just like Mom,
will find her very own Romeo
to free her from home,
to similar weed-wild days
of lunch-counter serving (this week),
retail stocking (next week),
too many (every week)
dishes, cats, bills, beers, job loss exhaustions.

Her guy'll come round
when it suits him
- give her a little, a wet and nice spray
near morning for the bloom she is, he'll coo
Oh baby, they're yours, those kids, but you're
my hybrid tea rose, more pretty from a distance,
the better to sniff at.

Little Girl Drowned

The day she flailed the water
the lifeguard was smoking off duty,
the lifelines snagged the dock.
No one was greatly surprised to find
the oxygen dead, the tank as empty
as her lungs were heavy.
Somebody snickered even,
and no one noticed,
and later they did as they had before:
The boats set out on the lake,
the children made ponds in the sand,
a lady painted the scenery.

The girl?
Who could imagine her then
a prima ballerina, a pure contralto,
a woman strong in labor?
Yes, and who could begrudge them routine
in their stunning grief -
those two old fishermen arthritic as trees?
No, nor the bums there who dozed on the beaches
with the water lapping sometimes
into their holes of mouths.

Volunteer Fire Department

Siren wails summon from town
clerks, stock boys, bartenders and hardware store salesmen.
They're joined by a clutch of area farmers,
and everyone's up now at the Cory Wilhelm place
where a smoldery leaf and rubbish pile
got wind of its own importance and skylarked hot
through too-dry grasses toward an ailing hen house.

Everything's snuffed pronto.
Elapsed time from first alert
to put-out: 20 minutes.

Still, everyone stays an hour,
fussing the chrome parts of the pumper,
stomping cold embers in tribal time-wasting.

When they leave they've
saved Cory's corn sheller that never worked right ever,
seen pictures of Justin Hobart's brand new baby,
and re-talked a poker round at the station house
three weeks before, after EMS training.

It's been a good fire.

Ritual   (for F., M. & H., A. & L.)

Yelps and shrieks, shrieks and yelps.
Tàpas, herring, and chèvre ravaged.
Paris bistro racket in a heartland living room.
At the core, Friday night people, six, in yappy discourse.

More hors d'oeuvres, tray two of beaded martinis
on the fast track to stomachs,
looser tongues passing paté and judgment
on local celebs. Someone is also toasting, no,
giving a Bronx cheer for Congress, the gin running low.

Now cometh a large Falstaffian meal
for these belt-loosening home guard regulars.
An argument rises and poofs over squash bisque.
Gossip drenches the hearts of palm salad.
Next: thoughts on a movie, confused with another,
wine-washed nostalgia salsa-ed by dirty jokes,
reports of the misspent days of a friend,
and as the cauliflower Mornay goes round again
invaluable tips for getting through
downtown Dubuque. Duluth? Whatever.

R.I.P. the pillaged entrée: wreck of lamb.

Dessert. A male delivers a big chest speech,
custardy flan the sole, wiggly listener.

Midnight. Coffee. Revival in lounge chairs.
Whew, no one next door has called the cops
for an excess guffaw violation.

Shoes back on, things collected,
a weary slow motion dance to the coat closet,
hugs near the door.

What shall we read next time? the book group asks.
What was the one tonight?

Edges

After the perturbations of coffee it starts.
Sectioning grapefruit calms her,
and she follows with:
Calendula - water,
Living room chairs - position,
Hallway painting - straighten.

But then she begins to slip,
slowly first, something misplaced - *in the desk, no. No!*
Abruptly then: torrents of daylight turning to glucose.
Stop it. Steady now.
I can sit here, control things, can . . .
She tries again: ritual, pattern, a note to a friend,
but halfway finished a stomach punch of chaos.
Yard's on fire. No, silly, of course not, but . . .

The bushes ignite, cool
in the sprinkler's arced cyclical sweep
till the firebomb sun through the window
screams in her eyes.

She gives in. Knick-knacks shatter,
irises die in thumb-and-forefinger meeting.
I did that?
Did it.
The walls slur toward her,
the rugs in chorus renew an argument.

Just the sentence of hours left,
the afternoon frayed with wonder
for long thin evenings swimming with doubt of
a night awash with steps not taken that might be.

The Massing of the Planets

(In June of 1991 astronomers noted that three planets were positioned
closer to one another over North America than they had been since
before the American Revolution. From ground level they appeared
to occupy a space no larger than that of a human fist at the end of an
extended arm.)

Over the neighbors' roof ridge in the pristine sky
of a mid-June twilight, the three arrive,
post-dinner guests commanding the evening,

Jupiter, cosmic Caesar
but shrunk in our local perspective
to laser-dot glint at the base of this astral V;

Venus, with diamond largesse, at right,
the radiant gypsy;

and Mars, the ember-fed leftist,
in the grey-to-blackening gouache of night.

They're rich relations we never dreamed being familial.
They've buried their quarrels to come together,
and they beam apologies for not dropping by
since old King George sent taxers
to thug our ancestor colonists.

Such good company!
As we pause in their steadying light
their aura claims us.
Mouths O-ed open, what shall we utter
of things these presences witnessed
on such enormous travels?

Gone too, in a mystery exit near midnight.

Nor would we compel them back,
their wonder dimming by too-sustained stay.

Neiman Marcus, The Spring Collection

Now strolling these chandeliered aisles -
the Gucci teens eye-shadowed chic
in Ecuador cottons and showcase silks,
the object young of St. Laurent.

They're all dressed up like cockatiels
with nothing to do but wander in riches,
to finger/toy with a hundred haute couture blouses
always with plenty of Rolex time,
poised on their five inch eel skin pumps
like breaths too rare for aspiration.

Stop. You in the de la Renta blouse, turn
to the one beside you. Ask: Lovely?
You at her side, with Coach bag reflecting
your mood, reply: Stunning!
Utter the words so they carefully graze
the mauve colored lipstick and thus give shading
to empty compliment.

Keep moving. Admire things. Buy,
your destiny free as your credit.
Acquire, since no one will pay you
notice as yesterday's you.
Have you looked to your surface
in the last few seconds?

Floor help are bringing you samples of die-proof youth.
You will never be old and in need of more than
a well-tailored something for dinner.

Try this pretty thing on. It's you.

Employee of the Month

Pump in overtime, yeah.
Pile up extra for payday night with the guys.

Or just go south after coffee break?
Not stop home? Punch out permanent?

Maybe get sick. Wimp on over to Howard the Clipboard:
It got me too, (snuffle, snuffle),
that bug that laid low Rita in LINENS.
Poor me, poor me: Jared limps off to the doc.

Maybe call Skeeter - that desk thing check on
in bonds and stocks he thinks he can wangle me.

Hell, stuff this, bum the coast at Dallas, fish a lot.

Or try some college here, third time, weekend classes.
Maybe get married?

Get some on-sale Gunk Gone for the pizza clogged drain.

Have some kids.

An Afternoon among the Politically Famous

You there in the catered mid-day light,
make words make phrases but carefully say
nothing say nothing well since
click since
someone may net your untethered comments
may inject them and spread them
like a germ-war contagion.

Judas has savored a canapé at your elbow.
Smile. Smile always
since it is long since
you were small town no one
and went unnoticed, went un-Nikoned.

Now you have you, you have
limos to glide in
streets named after you
click and
chic and
eyes of a dozen f-stops seeped in celluloid
teeth known everywhere
a hole
in the dailies
more checkbooks than memories
more aides than affectioned attachments
advancemen scoured of thoughts,
and here is a froth of a crowd to lift you.
Sit down click
relax click we will
click share
talk and

like two children on a rubbled playground
- on three: photo-op deep concern, please! -
confide our lives.

Young Teen Girls Saying Goodbye

A dazzle of hedged farewells,
a round-robin rite of exits stayed,
caught in motion this second with Ann saying bye,

to Lacy (teased, streaked hair)
and Jill (streaked hair teased)
and Jenny (teased hair streaked).

Ann's saying bye but fears now she slighted
her yesterday's heart reader, Sue,
so *Bye, hon'*, says Ann, to Sue again
before *Take care, Lorrie. Tomorrow, Jill?*

While turning (farewell in pirouette) Jill flutters
Bye, Ann and *Ciao, Chris* to her very best friend
this moment, but maybe this gushed goodbye,
she fears, sounds overly warm to Karen,
her lifetime secrets-confider, last month,
so Karen gets a repeat bye,
while she, with in-kind caution and affection,
sends round her very own soul-strong,
peeped out adieus to
never mind.

Has anyone bye-passed anyone?
(Lorrie to Karen? Jill to Jenny? Chris to Ann?)
Ah, someone at last has taken a step toward a door.
but another - Lacy - has also flashed on a purse forgotten,
so no one need actually commence a parting,
and soon, purse found, words will find throat again:
See you, Sue. You too, Lorrie . . . Karen.
Jill, call me, okay?
Ann, hey bye. Let's do this again.

Leaving the Farmers' Market

With our field fresh tomatoes
we will live to two hundred.

At Sunday dinner tomorrow this sweet corn
will bring together our warring cousins,
who, moaning in butter and kernels, will say
How could we ever have nursed such rancor?

Wasn't that Ike back there, disguised
as the sunflower vendor, revived and ready
to lead the country again?

A barn awaits us at home
sprung from the earth in place of the double garage.
Pitchforks and hoes on its stone foundation
summon our hands.

The Poet's Tell-All

Neglected, early on footloose,
        left to wander in glens of intuition.

Malformed, with a hunchback's freight of wonder,
        contorted delight for the small and unnoticed.

Scarred, too much imagination under the skin,
        crust skeins of non-conformity.

Bi-polar (chronic range of mind and
        dervish self-absorptions).

Struck, stammered
        by those too common for the common good.

Insane and untreatable: on-edge dream
        railings: all can be better than seems.

Richard Swanson lives in Madison, Wisconsin. After graduating from Rockford College and the University of Wisconsin, he taught English at Madison Area Technical College. He has published two previous books, novels (iUniverse): "Events of the Day," loosely based on the bombing of Sterling Hall in 1970, and "Brigid Does Bleak," a comedy about a sophisticated young woman in Chicago, who comes back to her small town roots in Wisconsin. "Men in the Nude in Socks" is his first poetry collection.